HOW TO
INTERVIEW
like a
Badass

The Comprehensive Guide to Finding
and Securing the Job of Your Dreams

LATOYA BALDWIN

How to Interview Like a Badass: The Comprehensive Guide to Finding and Securing the Job of Your Dreams
Published by ROBINSON ANDERSON PUBLISHING LLC
Frisco, Texas, U.S.A.

BALDWIN, LATOYA, Author
HOW TO INTERVIEW LIKE A BADASS
LATOYA BALDWIN

ISBN: 978-1-7358842-0-2

BUSINESS & ECONOMICS / Careers / Job Hunting

QUANTITY PURCHASES: Schools, companies, professional groups, clubs, and other organizations may qualify for special terms when ordering quantities of this title.
For information, email hello@latoyabaldwin.com.

Table of Contents

Introduction

> "The question isn't who is going to let me; it's who is going to stop me."
>
> —AYN RAND

Chances are, if this book has found its way into your life, you're preparing to make some pretty big career moves. It's exciting to have an opportunity to push yourself toward your higher purpose; to live the life you were always meant to! This also means you are on the cusp of a major life change. Change certainly can be scary, but rather than focusing on the uncertainties that lie ahead, let this be a reminder that this is your moment to take control of your destiny.

Whether you're up for a promotion at your current company, pivoting to a different industry to try something new, or you're rejoining the workforce after some time away, you already know that your experience and natural talents make you a certified badass.

You just might need a little guidance on how to showcase your greatness in the dreaded and, might I add, unneccesary stressful job interview process.

Most job interviews are not designed to put you in the hot seat, so to speak, but the reality is that companies need to assess your ability to perform the essential responsibilities of the job. Formal interviews are one of the most effective ways to qualify your fitness as it relates to the position you've applied for. After all, the best indicator of future success is past performance! Companies need to be sure that they are making a good investment in acquiring and promoting the best talent – at the same time, you deserve the chance to be sure that the position is the best fit for YOU.

As an HR executive and former Director of Talent Acquisition, I understand what major companies look for in top talent. The positions that I've held throughout the years have required me to both build and lead large teams – beginning with a formal interview process for each member. Over time, I have built a reputation for developing high performing teams and building creative recruiting strategies.

In short: I know what hiring managers are looking for and I want to help you exceed their expectations throughout the process. So, I have collected all of the information that you need to get hired and poured it into this book.

I am thrilled that you've met me here and we can have an open and honest conversation about what it takes to get hired in today's job market. The journey to where I am in my career today has been long and sometimes difficult. The thing is, I didn't have a guidebook that told me exactly how to grow my salary, reach my goals, and find the career of my dreams – I learned it all through trial and error; accepting feedback (a tool that I find invaluable) and observing others.

With this resource, you will know exactly how to optimize your job search, what you need to do to stand out to recruiters, and exactly how to prepare for your interview. You will better understand behavior-based interviews and why they are preferred. We will explore the STAR method for formatted interview answers, and how to negotiate your salary. You will know how to **interview like a badass.**

Are you ready to open your mind to all of the opportunity that life has to offer? We're going to start by discovering the right role for you. I believe that one of the reasons most people find themselves in search of a new position is because they are sitting in one that is not well-suited for them.

Chapter 1:

DISCOVERING THE RIGHT ROLE FOR YOU

"There is no passion to be found playing small—in settling for a life that is less than the one you are capable of living."

— NELSON MANDELA

When you're serious about your career and reaching your goals, you know that not just any position will suffice, and you might find yourself questioning whether or not you're on the right career path. It can be difficult to realize that the career you have (or desire) isn't right for you.

Let me tell you, it is so incredibly satisfying when you find your way and know that you are at the right place and time in your career. I believe that the first place to look is within. Once you've discovered what is it you want out of a role, you can move on to thinking about the larger picture of your career.

LEARNING YOUR PERSONALITY TYPE

I truly believe that a great way to get started on discovering the right role for you is by taking personality quizzes. It might not give you a definitive answer to the question, "what is the perfect job for me?", but it will help you determine what your strengths are.

There are many different kinds of personality quizzes out there from ones that you find in the back of Cosmo magazines to ones that were developed by psychologists to determine and predict how a person will function in a given scenario.

Although Cosmo quizzes are fun (I actually have one posted on my website!) these are not the type of personality quizzes I am talking about here.

Let's review five free self-assessment tests that will help you better understand yourself (and others) that you can take online. Some of them take a bit of time and a lot of honesty but they're all worth the investment if you're serious about the results. Use these to your advantage to help determine the work that best aligns with the insight you'll gain from these tools:

- **The Myers-Briggs Type Indicator.** This is an introspective question-naire that separates people into one of four categories: introversion or extraversion, sensing or intuition, thinking or feeling, judging or perceiving. Once you have been sorted into one of the categories, you can identify your specific personality type out of the 16 options.

- **The Keirsey Temperament Sorter.** Also an introspective question-naire, the Keirsey Temperament Sorter helps you determine roles that will be well-suited for you based on your personal temperament.

- **The Jungian Type Index.** This personality tests focuses more on the way that you think and what your psychological preferences are. It is another introspective personality quiz that could help determine a good role for you by explaining why and how you think the way you do.

- **The Fascination Personality Test.** This personality test is meant to identify not only the way that you view the world, but how the world views you! It breaks down the subtle cues you give off (intentionally or unintentionally) to determine how colleagues, customers, and leaders see you. You can build your career around the highest and best use of your personality.

- **The Enneagram Test.** There are nine numbers or "personalities" on the Enneagram scale. Each one deeply dives into your fears and motivations including the way you connect, how you understand others, the way you give and receive support, and how you accept things/others.

If you are still completely unsure what type of work is right for you, check out the online tool **MyNextMove.** It's a career assessment test sponsored by the U.S. Department of Labor to assist people in finding the career that they are best fit for.

In addition to evaluating the type of person that you are, it's crucial to map out your career path thus far.

Your career path is a series of positions that you will travel in and out of through the course of your career - unlike the generations before us who typically began in one position and stayed at the same company until they retired. There is nothing wrong with having multiple positions throughout your career, especially if each position is used as propulsion for new and greater heights. Stagnation is a career's worst enemy.

There are two general directions that a career path can go: vertically or laterally.

Some people choose to "move up" and seek out roles that advance their careers, while others may choose to seek out roles that are different, but equal in order to specialize or pivot their career path. The way that you move will ultimately be up to you! It will be determined by your career goals.

OUTLINING YOUR CAREER PATH

Here is a foolproof plan to discover the career path that is right for you:

1. OUTLINE YOUR CAREER GOALS

Write down and answer these questions and any others that you feel are pertinent to your specific career goals:

- What do I want out of my career?
- What are my values?
- What are my interests – both inside and outside of work?
- What are my strengths?

- What are my weaknesses?
- What kind of position am I looking for – a technical or specialized role, leadership position, etc.

2. CREATE A PLAN:

Life is marked by milestones. Birthdays, graduations, jobs, and weddings – there are always things we are striving for and reasons to celebrate when we attain them. Milestones help us know that we're on the right path.

Your career path should be marked with goals that you want to attain within the next two, five, and ten years. Make them as small and specific or large and broad as you want them to be, they just have to be realistic. Once you've laid out what you want to accomplish, research what you have to do to get the job done.

Career change? Apply for a promotion? Move to a new city? Write it all down!

3. RECALL YOUR PREVIOUS JOB EXPERIENCE

Your previous experience will be hugely helpful in determining your skillset as well as what makes you feel satisfied and fulfilled. Write down every position that you've ever held and what you liked/disliked about each. Here, you should also take note of the skillset that you exemplified in each position, what you learned while working there, and things that you were missing from each role.

4. INCLUDE YOUR INTERESTS

Write down everything that you enjoy doing both at work and at home – or wherever it is you like to do an activity. Your interests will help propel you into a position that you really love waking up to every day. When you find a role based on your passions, you are sure to find longevity in a position and be that much closer to living the life of your dreams.

5.   IDENTIFY YOUR VALUES

It's so important to find a role at a company that aligns with your values. This will help you find a career that you find fulfilling and one that you are truly passionate about. Write down a list of all the qualities that you find to be important in an employer and the environment that you'll be working in. Once you know exactly what it is that you're looking for, you'll have a better chance at finding it.

6.   CONSIDER COMPENSATION

Financially, what is it going to take for you to accomplish all of the goals in your two, five, and ten-year plans? Adjust your salary goals for the stage of your career path that you're in by determining exactly what is an acceptable starting point and how much you'll need your salary to go in a certain amount of time. Finally, discover whether or not there are enough growth opportunities in the positions that you are considering. Always keep your future goals in mind.

Once you've outlined what the right role looks like for you, it's time to begin the job search.

Chapter 2:

EFFICIENT JOB SEARCH TECHNIQUES

"The only way to do great work is to love what you do. If you haven't found it yet, keep looking. Don't settle."

— STEVE JOBS

Searching and applying for new jobs isn't as easy as just that anymore. You have to be active, relentless, and know how to stand out from the crowd. It's the only way you're going to land a job in today's competitive job market that is largely driven by who you know – your *network*.

Putting yourself out there, being vulnerable enough to let people get to know you, and asking for help when you need it might not be what you're used to in a job search. But, then again, that's why you're here right? To learn something new and take your career to places it's never been before!

I know that hunting around for the perfect position can be tough so let's get into some ways to make the entire process a little bit easier.

TAKE A GOOD LOOK AT YOUR CURRENT COMPANY

Start by remembering why you came into this position in the first place. The key here is to assess all of the things that you love about your current position and the company that it is settled in – and the things that you wish you had more of. If you think that you can find what you're looking for in your company elsewhere, it's time to start searching for other opportunities!

There may also be the case that the company simply no longer aligns with your personal values. If you've decided that the culture is no longer one that helps you be your best self, it sounds like it could be time to find a company better suited for your needs. This brings me to the next point.

SEEK OUT COMPANIES THAT ALIGN WITH YOUR VALUES

If you're taking the plunge and leaving a position, chances are you're not going to want to land a position just to be in search of another one in a few months. Leaving a company that you're familiar with to start with a new one is a huge decision and your next step should be calculated.

Read job descriptions carefully and apply only for positions that you think will foster your success – not just the first few that show up because you're itching for a new job.

Go beyond the information that you glean from recruiters and the basic information that is easily attainable on the application page. In the next part of this chapter, we'll go more in-depth on how to research a company to make sure they align with what you're looking for.

CREATE A "HUMBLE-BRAG PORTFOLIO"

The proper term for this is "job-search portfolio," but I prefer to call it what it is. One of the easiest ways to stand out to potential employers is to offer something that no other applicant has. So, show yourself off!

Many people think that portfolios are reserved for the creative industry (artists, designers, etc.) but they can be used in any job search! Your humble-brag portfolio will include hard proof that you have all of the skills and characteristics that you say you do and should be organized as such:

1. **Title page** with your name and contact information
2. **Statement** of originality and **request** that the work not be copied without permission
3. **Table of contents** to make information easy to find. Chapters should be separated by dividers
4. **Mission statement** that is no longer than four sentences
5. **Career goals**
6. **Resume & business cards**
7. **Degrees, certifications, and awards** this may include any press coverage you have received
8. **Skills & abilities** as they pertain to the position you are applying for
9. **References**

As portfolios are not as expected as resumes are, you should have a note at the bottom of your resume that reads, "references and professional portfolio available upon request."

Your portfolio should be inserted into a professional three-ring binder that has a zipper and is made out of vinyl, leather, or fabric.

At the top of your interview, ask permission to share your portfolio. You should refer to it when appropriate; using its contents to support your answer. If done right, this will aid you in showcasing yourself as the best candidate for the job. Don't overdo it though, I'd recommend referencing the portfolio no more than 2-3 times throughout the course of the interview. Also, waiting until the end of the interview may take up too much time and put some of your accomplishments out of context.

ATTEND JOB FAIRS AND CAREER EXPOS

One of the best ways to find a position that is perfect for you is to get a sample of the company at a job fair. If you hear of one coming up in your area, or know of one coming up online, do plenty of research beforehand and pick out the companies that you are interested in.

Virtual job fairs are becoming more and more popular as much of the world transitioned to working from home early in 2020. In fact, CNBC reported in August 2020 that 80% of recruiting will be virtual for the foreseeable future.

It can take as little as one minute to make a lasting impression on a person. A day spent at a job fair has the potential to fill your pockets or email inbox with opportunities that you can refer to the next time you're in search of one.

Job fairs and career expos can be a bit overwhelming so here are my top tips for attending them:

- Get a map of the floorplan (usually at the door) and highlight/circle the booths that you want to visit.
    - For virtual job fairs, there is usually a meeting room schedule posted ahead of time. Print out the schedule and highlight the "rooms" that you want to attend.
- Print out at least 20 copies of your resume and carry them in a professional-looking folder, briefcase, or bag.
    - For virtual job fairs, you may be required to submit your resume online to all of the participating employers.
- Speak directly to the recruiter or hiring manager.
- Have an elevator pitch ready (what's an elevator pitch? We'll get there!)
- Collect contact information from whomever you talk to.
- Follow up with an email saying how nice it was to meet them, that you're excited about the position, and redistribute your resume electronically if needed.
- In about a week or so, follow up again with a phone call to inquire if the position is still available or not.

BE IN RUTHLESS PURSUIT OF YOUR DREAMS.

Don't give up after one job fair or a few weeks of looking. The right position might be closer than you think or come around when you least expect it! The truth is that the best way to predict the future is to create it. Envision yourself in a position that you love and keep working until you're in it.

Always be on the lookout for new opportunities, keep learning and trying to be the best version of yourself that you can be. Ask for feedback whenever possible and use it to be better next time! Past interviews where things did not go as expected can help you understand what to course correct.

Once you fully understand the type of career that is best for your personality, and you've got your career goals mapped out, it's time to find a company that offers what you're looking for. The research process should be carried out meticulously so that you can make the best-informed decision about where you send your resume to.

GATHERING INFORMATION ON A COMPANY

It's important to know how to effectively research a company during the job hunt process so you can narrow your focus and only apply to the positions that are the best fit. It also helps when you're going to job fairs, as previously stated. Job fairs can be large and overwhelming so having a plan and some background information on the companies that you want to talk to is the way to go.

Quite frankly, doing your research and knowing a bit about the company is a basic expectation of recruiters. It's not just about a company assessing your ability to join their team, you should be equally invested in evaluating if the company is best suited for you. No one will know that better than you.

So, how do you know for sure that a company is a good match for you? Research, critical thinking, and some self-reflection. You can start by going to a company's website and reading through every page.

Read their testimonial page if they have one to see what their community thinks about them. Look at the staff biographies to get an understanding of if you'll be compatible with prospective colleagues. Search for their mission statement and core values. If they are a publicly-traded company you can also find the earnings statements. Profitability is a good indicator of that company's potential longevity.

Once you've finished pouring over their website, head for their social media accounts. This can help to give you a better idea of what the day-to-day operations of a company look like and give you a better insight into their general brand.

After you feel like you've done as much research as possible, ask yourself these questions:

DO I SHARE A PURPOSE WITH THIS COMPANY?

Your work has meaning. Every day that you wake up, put on your power suit, and walk out the door; you have a purpose. If your purpose in life and work is not aligned with that of the company that you're thinking about working for, it probably won't be a long-term engagement. You deserve to walk into and leave work with your head held high, knowing that what you've accomplished within your organization is making an impact.

DOES THE CULTURE ALIGN WITH MY VALUES?

These days, a lot of companies tout that they have "awesome culture around the office," or something along those lines. The thing is, one person's idea of what awesome culture is, isn't necessarily another's. Some people want to work in a laid-back environment that has happy hour on Fridays while others crave a more professional setting.

And then there's the aspect of diversity, teamwork, communication, etc. There are too many factors that go into a company's culture to just boil it down and define it by the word "awesome." It'll be up to you to figure out YOUR idea of "awesome culture" and make sure that the company you're looking at fits into that idea.

HOW DOES IT FIT INTO MY LIFE?

One reason people are often unhappy at work or settle for less is because they view their job as something separate from their lives. They know who they are outside of work and think that as long as they get their work done with little to no issue, they can get to living as soon as 5 o'clock hits.

It's crucial to realize that your job is a key part of your life. You spend one-third of your week at work so it should be able to fit nicely into your life so that you are energized for work each morning, glad to spend 8+ hours there, and still have energy to participate in activities afterwards.

If you're taking a more demanding position, you should also consider whether or not you are going to have to sacrifice friend or family time, the commute, weekend and holiday hours, vacation time, etc. Will the extra responsibility and sacrifices be worth it to you?

WHY DO I WANT TO WORK HERE?

Take the compensation package out of the equation for a second. Would you still want to work for that company? Is it going to offer you things that are almost as fulfilling as your paycheck? Of course, we all go to work because we want and need money, but since you're spending nearly one-third of your week at work, you should choose a company that has more to offer than monetary compensation.

How do they view problem-solving? Will you have more chances to do the kind of work that you really love to do? Will you be an integral part of a team or get the chance to lead one? If you can't answer why you want to work at a specific company without mentioning the compensation package, it might be in your best interest to consider another option.

When looking at a new company, it's not only important for it to have an effective leader, but the leader should be one that you would take pride in following and learning from. Much of your future could be determined by whoever is leading you there and if you don't trust them to pave the way, scratch them off your list as well.

You might be able to gather intel on a leader by reaching out to people who work at the company already. If you can get in touch with a potential colleague, see if you can't take them out for coffee or a cocktail and pick their brain. If they reassure you that they trust their leader to lead them to success, you know you're on the right track.

Speaking of communicating with fellow professionals... let's learn how to build and leverage a professional network, shall we?

CULTIVATING A PROFESSIONAL NETWORK

Your professional network is invaluable. They're the people who you learn from, offer your services to and make other connections that will further your career. Digital media has certainly changed the way that we cultivate and maintain professional networks, but it hasn't made them any less important.

It becomes all too easy to communicate with the people in our network through email, chat and text message, but it's crucial to not lose sight of the importance of a face-to-face conversation. Even a video call every now and again will help to strengthen your connection with someone and give all parties an idea of what you can do for each other.

Cultivating a professional network can be tough if you don't know where to start, so here's your 5-step plan:

1. Figure out what you want from your professional network
2. Put yourself out there
3. Consider the network you already have
4. Look within your company
5. Have something great to offer

FIGURING OUT WHAT YOU WANT

What are you looking for in a professional network? Job offers? Sales leads? Mentorship? Once you've figured out what you're looking for, you can start positioning yourself to meet your network halfway.

Think about the people that you already know – or know of – and write down a list of the people that you want to get to know better and why. These could be people in your office, your boss, your boss's boss, or potential mentors. Keep your list realistic – under 10 – and determine ways of communicating with them that will work for all parties involved (email chain, monthly networking "event" at a local restaurant, one-on-one time, etc.).

PUTTING YOURSELF OUT THERE

When you're building a relationship of any kind, the key is authenticity. Be yourself and act naturally – discuss things that you're interested in and find someone that you have common ground with that you can build off of.

One of the most traditional ways of building out your professional network is at networking events. Although 2020 has put a halt to gatherings, there are still plenty of ways to meet new people and have valuable conversations online, but don't toss traditional networking events aside completely. They're not only valuable, but they can be a bit of fun once you get comfortable with the crowd.

In the meantime, check out LinkedIn groups – local, national, and international ones – and join ones that you're interested in. Joining usually takes just a click of a button – sometimes a short survey – and you've got a large network at your disposal before you know it. After you've joined, it's up to you to find the individuals that you can strengthen connections with. If you've joined a local group, see if you can start a weekly zoom session for everyone to get to know each other better.

CONSIDERING YOUR CURRENT NETWORK

The next time you're at a social gathering, there's no harm in mentioning your work if the topic comes up. You might be standing in the room with someone who can open just the door that you're looking for.

Don't take the people that you already know for granted. When you consider the people, who live in your building, previous employers, your friend's family members, and favorite teachers, you might have a bigger professional network than you think.

LOOKING WITHIN YOUR COMPANY

It's not unheard of for leaders to recommend their team members for other positions if they've outgrown their current one. If you're looking to rise up and you have a leader with whom you feel you can have that conversation with, they might just be able to point you in the right direction.

If your company practices team building, use those opportunities to talk to your colleagues and adopt them into your network, too. You never know what someone in another department could do for you.

HAVING SOMETHING TO OFFER

When you bring people into your professional network, you have to realize that you're also becoming a part of theirs. Instead of asking someone to have a conversation with you so that you can pick their brain, offer to assist them with a project.

You would do well to learn something new while you're in the process of cultivating your professional network. Often times, we hit dead ends because we've surrounded ourselves with too many like-minded individuals. It's important to have diversity in your network and be able to offer a wide range of skills so that you can adapt to whomever needs you AND so that you can find what you're looking for.

Chapter 3:

FIRST IMPRESSIONS

"You never get a second chance
to make a first impression."

—WILL ROGERS

Many people struggle with their resumes and cover letters. It's tough to get all of your best qualities down on paper, format it properly, and make sure the language is on point. That being said, your resume is the first point of interaction with any recruiter or company so it should be crafted in a way that portrays an accurate and attractive image of you. Whether a professional or personal horizon, every impression counts, and your resume is a chance to make a memorable first impression to lead you towards your dream job.

WRITING A WINNING RESUME

Your resume should perfectly summarize your qualifications as a job candidate. The goal of most resumes is to explain 4 major things about a job candidate:

1. **Educational history:** your highest degrees should be listed on your resume as well as the ones that are relevant to the position that you're applying for. For example, if you have a master's and undergraduate degree that are both applicable to the position that you're applying for, include them both.

2. **Applicable skills:** The skills listed on your resume will show recruiters and hiring managers that you've got what it takes to excel in the position that you're applying for. You will find what they're looking for by analyzing the job description.

3. **Summary of qualifications:** Your summary should be easily scannable and highlight the best parts of your career so far. Include official certification and awards as well as quantifiable achievements like how you cut down costs by 25% or gained X number of new clients for your firm in record-breaking time.

4. **Professional memberships:** List any relevant clubs or associations that you belong to or are on the board of. For example, if you are a journalist applying to a newspaper, they might like to know that you're a member of the Society of Professional Journalists.

PRESENTATION IS EVERYTHING

The way you design and present your resume is critical. Use aesthetically pleasing but simple designs that provide recruiters ease in reviewing it. Don't use different fonts, colors, tables and icons unless there is specific requirement; instead utilize spacing, heading and sections properly to make it easy to consume. Your resume should have a balanced layout with appropriate white space.

- **Check your grammar.** All too often resumes are completed with inconsistent comma use. There are two ways to write out a list with commas: "one, two, and three" or "one, two and three." Technically, either one can be used, but it's important that you use the same structure throughout your resume.

- **Space your text consistently.** You might be surprised to learn that some people have an eye for an extra space between words or paragraphs. If you have inconsistencies in your spacing, it could be quite distracting to the reader.

- **Choose your font wisely**. The standard-sized font is 10-12 point with a professional design. Sans serif is the choice (think Ariel or Tahoma) for digital copies while serif (think Times New Roman) is optimal for print copies. Your font should be consistent throughout the document with the exception of your heading and resume section titles which may appear larger (size 14-16 and 13-14, respectively).

- **Measure margins**. Make sure your margins are the same size to the left and right and top to bottom. Half-inch to one inch is recommended.

- **Check your alignments**. Even word processors aren't perfect all the time. Sometimes a setting gets changed without the user realizing it and bullets or tabs are thrown out of alignment.

- **Overall consistency**. If you typed out your job title in bold in your first listing, it should be presented as bold throughout your other listings as well. Check to make sure every alteration that you've made to text was done so with intention.

- **Honesty**. It can be tempting to say that you're an iMovie expert because you recall being proficient in college. However, if this topic comes up during the interview and you can't tell them exactly what makes you an expert, you might cost yourself the job.

SHOWCASE YOURSELF AND YOUR CORE COMPETENCIES

The recruiter wants to know how well you have done your job in the past to draw conclusions about what you can deliver in the position you are seeking. Write a concise summary describing who you are and what you have done professionally, coupled with a few personal attributes.

Your profile should be followed by a skills and core competencies section to clearly highlight your abilities along with evidence of accomplishments in 1-2 sentences. Your core competencies are the skills that make you a perfect candidate for the position.

After your profile, there should be a small section that lists your core competencies in bullet form. More advanced resumes will have a rating system for their core competencies in which there are five or so circles that are filled in according to their personal understanding. For example, if you have an excellent understanding of project management, you would have all five of the circles filled in. If you have a good understanding of risk management, you would have three or four of the circles filled in. This format is not required but it may give a resume a competitive edge.

MAKE AN IMPACT WITH EXPERIENCE

Your experience is one of the most important parts of your resume because it's the basis by which your relevance and suitability for the role is graded. Many recruiters may head straight for this section first to determine whether or not you have the experience and skills to be considered for the position.

The experience section of your resume should list professional positions you've held including the dates of which you were employed, your title(s) employer(s), skills, and accomplishments.

- **Companies you worked for**: Your most recent employer should be listed first with their full and official name followed by your previous employer, and so on. This section should be fresh and relevant with employment that has taken place within the last 10-years or three employers.

- **Locations of the companies**: You don't need to list their exact address, but the city and state of your job should be apparent.

- **Employment dates**: The standard date format for resumes is the month and year you began working in a position and the month and year you left.

- **Job titles**: Be as specific as possible about your job title but don't use acronyms to describe them. Industry-specific jargon should not be found on a professional resume.

- **Responsibilities and impact**: In 3-5 bullets, explain your responsibilities and connect them to your successes. For example: "responsible for building high-performance teams and increased productivity by 15%."

- **Promotions**: Showing that you were valued at your last position and performed so well that you rose up in the ranks will make you an attractive candidate.

- **Awards and recognitions**: You may either choose to list your awards and/or recognitions that you've received underneath the job description or in a separate section. Quantify your achievements with realistic figures and numbers wherever possible (e.g. your GPA).

KEYWORDS MATTER

Keywords in your resume help to tailor your resume for the specific job that you're applying for. Keywords are skills, credentials, abilities – words that are going to stand out to a recruiter or hiring manager. Some companies also use "smart" job seekers to digitally scan resumes and applications for relevant keywords. The more often you have the keywords, that they're looking for, the more likely you'll get chosen for review by hand.

Utilize relevant and powerful keywords in your experience, skills and profile summary. This should be modified with each individual application to ensure they are relevant to the job that you're applying for. Do not load your resume with too many keywords, words that aren't required for the job, or words that are too technical. Remember, no company specific jargon.

You can find the keywords that are relevant to your position by looking at the job description. The job listing will tell you exactly what recruiters and hiring managers are looking for, so you know what to include on your resume.

Make sure to be as specific as possible so recruiters know exactly how a keyword relates to your skills. For example, the term "marketing" could mean too many things. Perhaps "social media marketing," or "Chief Marketing Officer" would be more appropriate for describing what your position was.

ACCURATE CONTACT INFORMATION

Double and triple check your contact information! Recruiters will reach you through available contact information on your resume. Ensure that it's accurate and you can be reached at the given email address or phone number.

The email address you list on your resume should be professional – not your favorite band from high school or a silly nickname. Create a separate one for your job search if needed and stick with a variation of your first name/initial and last name/initial. If you have to add numbers, make them appropriate and few.

MAKE A LASTING IMPRESSION

In the end, your resume is all about creating a memorable impression and drawing the company's interest in to deepen their association with you as a candidate. If not for a current position, ideally it should be one to remember and marked in their recruiting database for future openings.

You will be able to make a lasting impression by having an excellent format, keeping your eye out for any inconsistencies, succinct writing, the correct keywords, and having a captivating cover letter.

BEST PRACTICES FOR COVER LETTER WRITING

A cover letter is a one-page brief that should not only entice the recruiter to review your resume but will give you an advantage over other candidates who would be applying without a cover letter. Many applicants overlook the cover letter as just an unnecessary additional document. While it might not be necessary to join the application process, it can only help make you look more prepared to showcase your skills. A cover letter should be an essential part of your job application and should always be sent.

Your cover letter should:

- Highlight your strengths and accomplishments along with your relevance for the role.
- Elaborate your expression of interest to work for the company
- Give the reader insight into who you are and how you work
- Tell a compelling story
- Provide recruiters a call to action.

Your cover letter aims to complete a lot in a very little amount of space and time, so your word choice is absolutely critical. When deciding which skills that you'd like to highlight, it might be helpful to make a Venn diagram with the skills that you have and the skills that the job description lists. The shared skills will be the ones that you choose to highlight in your cover letter. Because you have such a limited amount of words to make a killer impression, stick to 2-3 skills for your cover letter.

Here are a few guidelines for a writing a cover letter that will grab recruiter's attention:

CONTACT DETAILS AND ADDRESSEE

Start your cover letter by providing contact details clearly at the top, mentioning your name, email address, contact number, and mailing address. As we shift to a more digital world, placing your LinkedIn profile link here has become common practice. This adds to your credibility as recruiters can quickly access more information about you as well as your professional network.

Address the recruiter by name if you have it. Sometimes, the name will be available in the job advertisement or email address. However, if you aren't sure, then address them as "Dear Hiring Manager," or "Dear Recruiter." Do not use "Dear Sir/Madam" and refrain from "To whom it may concern" as it is outdated.

Addressing the reader properly is very important because it's their very first impression of you. If you improperly address them, you may risk offending them and cost yourself an interview.

STRUCTURE AND TONE

The structure of well written cover letter is essential. Structure your letter properly in paragraphs to provide recruiters with ease in consuming the included information. Neat and simple aesthetics are always appreciated – they should match the tone of your resume that is to follow with balanced white space and text.

The tone of your writing might vary from company to company, but overall, it should be professional and formal. Your research into the company should be able to help you determine the tone that you write in.

Overall, the structure and tone should flow naturally and sound like you are speaking directly to the reader. It should not, however, be so casual that it reads like you are speaking to a friend.

THE OPENING PARAGRAPH

Your first paragraph needs to make a great introduction and encourage the recruiter to keep reading. It should highlight your accomplishments along with your interest in joining the company. Provide persuasive and logical reasons for your interest rather than generic statements - interests rooted in the company's mission or values are most impactful.

Try to match the company's vision and mission with your personal goals and ambitions to make an impression. The more relevance, personalization and interest you create, the higher the chances that the recruiter will move on to your resume.

THE SECOND PARAGRAPH

The second paragraph, or the "Power Paragraph," of your cover letter is what hooks the reader onto you. It should address job requirements and responsibilities as posted by the company with an explanation of how you are the best fit for the position. By the end of this paragraph, the reader should know why you are the best candidate for the job.

Here is where you will showcase your previous work experience, skills and achievements by aligning relevance with the advertised position. The keywords and required skills from the job description should be mentioned in this paragraph to build a strong case.

Remember to expand on the keywords that you mention; "Excellent leadership skills" will not be enough here. Give a succinct example that perfectly showcases how you have been an excellent leader in the past.

THE THIRD PARAGRAPH

Prove to the recruiter that you have done your due diligence and have some knowledge about the company. Recruiters are interested to understand how you would contribute to the success of the role and company so illustrate this clearly.

Explain how you would leverage your transferable skills and experiences to fulfill the requirements of the advertised position – refer back to the skill(s) that you mentioned in the second paragraph.

CLOSING

Your cover letter closing matters so make it as strong as the rest of your anecdote. It should provide a convincing "call to action" for recruiters to review your resume – further shortlisting your application in the process.

You should prompt the reader to contact you for an interview – not the other way around. Closing with a promise such as, "I will be in touch to schedule an interview" is presumptuous and crosses a line. The reader may find this quite impolite and move on to the next letter.

Make sure to offer thanks for their time and consideration, and chose a professional closing such as, "Sincerely," "Best Regards," or "Thank you for your consideration." Let them know what you're excited to speak with them further about the position and to share more information about yourself.

AVOID OVERUSED WORDS AND PHRASES

Remember that recruiters and hiring managers are going to read hundreds, if not, thousands of cover letters in their days. Yours will stand out if you avoid using language that is commonly found in cover letters

- "Thank you for taking the time to look at my resume"
- "I believe my skillset makes me a perfect candidate for this job"
- "heavy-lifting"
- "game-changer"
- "Think outside the box"
- "I'm not sure if you are aware"
- "dynamic"
- "Please feel free"
- "significant"
- "Self-Starter,"
- "Detail-Oriented"
- "Forward-Thinker"

Leaving out these words and phrases will push you to be more original in your writing and impress recruiters who are tired of reading similar cover pages all day.

Now, you can only get so far in an interview with a cover letter and resume. While your accomplishments and credentials will certainly get your foot in the door, the other half of killing it in the interview process is showing off your personality and letting the person interviewing you get to know you. Since you only have a small timeframe, you'll have to have a great elevator pitch.

CRAFTING YOUR ELEVATOR PITCH

Essentially, your elevator pitch is going to be a summary of your cover letter and resume. It's called an "elevator pitch" because it should be so concise that you can give it from beginning to end in the time that it would take you to complete an elevator ride.

The few sentences that you choose to include in your elevator pitch should effectively communicate who you are and what your goals are to someone who has never met you before.

When an elevator pitch is crafted and executed well, it can help you build your professional network, get you the job you're vying for, and connect with your new colleagues on your first day of work. It's always tough to be the newest member of a team, but if you've got your personal introduction at the ready, you'll have one less thing to worry about.

USING AN ELEVATOR PITCH

There's almost no professional situation that you'll find yourself in where an elevator pitch is inappropriate. You can use it on the job hunt, at job fairs and expos, networking events, in job interviews, or in actual elevators! This works to establish rapport with interviewers or recruiters because you're giving them a quick, high-level view of your experience while adding a few personal things.

The thing is, a cover letter and resume can only get you so far – the rest of it is going to be up to your personality. Your elevator pitch gives you the chance to let your qualifications and personality shine.

When you're in a job interview or meeting someone for the first time, people want to get to know you right off the bat, so they'll likely ask you a question like, "what do you do?" or ask you to tell them about yourself.

Some people's mind tends to go blank after this prompt. In fact, it's not uncommon at all! This is exactly why elevator pitches are so important: even if your nerves take over, you'll have a few well-rehearsed sentences at the ready.

A well-crafted elevator pitch:

- Should be under two minutes long
- Is compelling and persuasive
- Lists your skills and accomplishments
- Is well-rehearsed, but spoken naturally
- Ends with a business card handout (as long as you aren't in an interview)
- Leaves a memorable impression

ELEVATOR PITCH TEMPLATE

All great elevator pitches are structured the same way. They should be short, to the point, and give the person you're talking to a pretty good idea of who you are by the time you're done pitching.

If it's helpful to you, copy the text below to a Word or Google doc and fill in the blanks with your own answers. These 7 steps will be the foundation of your 90-second introduction. Absolutely adjust the framework for your elevator pitch as it makes sense for your situation.

5. I am [NAME]
6. I grew up in [CITY, STATE]
7. I earned my [DEGREE] at [COLLEGE/UNIVERSITY]. GO ____!
8. While in school I [EXTRACIRRUCULAR, INTEREST OR FOCUS]
9. After graduating, I was a [POSITION] at [FIRST EMPLOYER OUT OF SCHOOL] and was responsible for [1-2 CORE ROLES]. I spent the following [# OF MONTHS/YEARS] working at [BRIEFLY HIGHLIGHT JOB HISTORY WITH NAME OF COMPANY(S) AND POSITION(S)]. Currently, I am a [POSITION] at [EMPLOYER] where I [#1 THING YOU DO].

10. One thing I am most proud of [BEST ACHIEVEMENT IN CURRENT OR PREVIOUS ROLE]
11. When I am not working, I am [1-2 HOBBIES OR INTERESTING FACT]

PRACTICE, PRACTICE, PRACTICE

After you've got your elevator pitch outlined, practice it until it's perfect. Chances are, you'll want to tweak it a few times, try out a couple different options for your solutions to problems, and the closing call to action. Practice by speaking your pitch out loud to yourself, record yourself saying it so you can hear how it sounds, and bounce some ideas off of others that you respect.

Your elevator pitch is what you're going to use to capture the attention of the person that you're talking to. A successful elevator pitch will result in a conversation on the spot or, hopefully, an interview! Prepare yourself for the interview by cultivating power stories that make you undeniably impressive to the person you're speaking with.

By now, you are so close to knowing that you're going to nail that interview. You've found a position at a company that is a perfect fit, you have a very impressive cover letter and resume, you've written and rehearsed your elevator speech so that you're practically mumbling it in your sleep.

All of that preparation will get you confidently through the door and past the introductory period of the interview. But you don't want to be caught off guard with what comes next:

"Tell me about a time when..."

Chapter 4:

BEHAVIOR-BASED INTERVIEWS

> "The most beautiful thing you
> can wear is confidence."
>
> —BLAKE LIVELY

Behavior-Based Interviews ask you to recall a certain time in your professional or personal life that relates to your qualifications for the job. These interviews focus less on your qualifications themselves and more on the way that you put your qualifications into action.

You can prepare for Behavior-Based Interviews by cultivating power stories and utilizing the STAR Method.

POWER STORIES

When we sit down and try, we all can think of past situations where we excelled at a given task or project, went above and beyond to solve a problem and/or made an impact on someone or a company. Those situations should be chronicled (like a rolodex) to capture these past experiences. As long as you are not completely switching industries, these situations become power stories and can be easily tailored to fit any question.

The common scenarios that interviewers are looking for are hiding in plain sight within the job description. Studying the position carefully and considering your skills and talents will help save you from that moment of panic that comes after their question and before your answer.

Power stories can be easily formulated by following the STAR interview response method which is outlined in the next section. Using this method will tell you exactly how to create and share a story in a concise manner without sounding like you're boasting about your accomplishments.

THE STAR INTERVIEW RESPONSE METHOD

The STAR interview response method will help you come up with concrete examples to an interviewer's questions and prompts. When you've got about 7-8 power stories in your rolodex that perfectly exemplify the fact that you've got the skills it takes to nail the job, you're in great shape for the interview.

"Share an example of a situation where..."

1. **Situation**: Set the scene for your example by briefly explaining the context of the situation. Your situation should be as specific as possible and be relevant to what the interviewer is asking.

2. **Task**: Next, describe the specific challenge or task that relates to the question and your responsibility in the scenario. Perhaps you were practicing conflict resolution or asked to work on a seemingly impossible deadline.

3. **Action**: You then explain exactly what steps you took to accomplish the task to rose to meet the challenge. At this part of the story, focus on what you accomplished, rather than your team or boss.

4. **Result**: Finally, share what positive outcomes your actions achieved.

This simple framework will help you tell meaningful stories about previous work experiences. By employing all four steps, you will thereby provide a comprehensive answer.

STAR INTERVIEW RESPONSE METHOD IN PRACTICE

The Interviewer Says: *"Tell me about a time when you had to complete a task within a tight deadline."*

Your Response:

Situation: *"In my previous sales role at XYZ, I was put in charge of the transfer to an entirely new client management system—on top of handling my daily sales calls and responsibilities."*

Task: *"The goal was to have the transition to the new database completed within six weeks, without letting any of my own sales numbers slip below my targets."*

Action: *"In order to do that, I had to be very careful about how I managed all of my time. So, I blocked off an hour each day on my calendar to dedicate solely to the migration to the new platform. During that time, I worked on transferring the data, as well as cleaning out old contacts and updating outdated information. Doing this gave me enough time to chip away at that project, while still handling my normal tasks."*

Result: *"As a result, the transfer was completed two weeks ahead of the deadline and I finished the quarter 15% ahead of my sales goal."*

COMMON BEHAVIORAL-BASED INTERVIEW QUESTIONS

POSSIBLE QUESTIONS YOU MUST BE PREPARED TO ANSWER:

Each response should be no more than 3-minutes long.

Tell me about yourself.

Why do you want to work here?

Why should we hire you?

Tell me about your strengths and weaknesses.

Tell me about a time you disagreed with a decision. What did you do?

Tell me about a time you made a mistake.

Tell me about a time when you used your problem-solving skills to find a solution to a problem.

Share an example of how you were able to motivate a coworker, your peers or your team.

Why are you leaving your current job?

Why was there a gap in your employment history?

Can you talk about a time you had to make a decision with limited information? How did you determine what would be the best decision?

How would your boss and coworkers describe you?

What do you like to do outside of work?

Give an example of an unpopular decision you've made, what the result was, and how you managed it.

Can you describe a time when you experienced rapid change? How did you handle the situation?

Tell me about a goal you failed to achieve.

Can you describe a time when a team member wasn't doing their work? What did you do?

How do you prioritize your work?

Can you describe a time when you went out of your way to please a customer?

What are your salary requirements?

What questions do you have for me?

PREPARING YOUR STAR INTERVIEW RESPONSE METHODS

Although you won't know the interview questions or method ahead of time, most behavioral interviews will focus on various work-related challenges that demonstrate critical thinking and problem-solving, as well as situations that showcase leadership skills, conflict resolution, and performance under pressure.

To prepare for your interview, review the job description and required skills. Consider what sort of challenges might arise or what obstacles you may have to navigate in the position.

Then, make a list of the various situations you've handled in your past work experience that would display the strengths you'll need to succeed in the role.

- Prepare a list of competencies required for the job either by reviewing job descriptions or researching the internet.
- Write down 7-8 specific examples of occasions where those skills were exhibited by you in past work experiences.
- For each example, notate the Situation, Task, Action, and Result.

Chapter 5:

PREPARING FOR THE INTERVIEW

"Confidence comes from knowing what you're doing. If you are prepared for something, you usually do it. If not, you usually fall flat on your face."

—TOM LANDRY

During a job interview, you may be asked tough questions. Preparing well-thought-out answers ahead of time will significantly reduce the risk of responding with the first – and not likely best – answer. Sitting in silence for 15 seconds to think of an answer feels like forever.

Quickly responding with your best answer will show that you are well-prepared and will increase the interviewers' confidence in your ability to do the job. In addition to these questions, be prepared for a few role-specific or technical questions.

BEST PRACTICES

It's normal to feel anxious the day before a big interview, but properly preparing is crucial. In fact, employability is directly correlated to preparation but only 1 in 10 candidates actually spend two or more hours preparing.

Get yourself a leg up on the competition by beginning to prepare as soon as you hear about the interview, or at least 4-5 days in advance. When it comes down to the day before the interview, you will be well-rehearsed and confident in your ability to ace it.

In the 24-hours before an interview, absolutely anything could happen – having to stay late at work, run last minute errands, who knows! Leaving that last day for prep will make you feel crammed and rushed and leave you wondering if you've actually done all the preparing that you needed to.

Give yourself those 24-hours beforehand to calm your nerves and reassure yourself that you are a badass and you are ready for this!

Aim to practice 1-2 of these items every day leading up to the interview; starting with #1 and working your way down:

1. Research the company
2. Review the role
3. Practice with a mock interview
4. Prepare questions for the interviewer
5. Look the part
6. Plan the commute/video call
7. Exhibit positive body language

8. Respond with honest answers

9. Send a thank you email

Once you have made an impression with your resume and earned an interview, your execution of the interview will determine your success in landing your dream job. Essentially, the interview is the process that will define whether you are selected or rejected. Many candidates take interview preparation for granted resulting in their failure during the process. Regardless of your experience and personal mastery, you always need to prepare yourself for the interview. Here are several tips to help you be more prepared for the interview process.

RESEARCH THE COMPANY

Once you have received an interview call it is time to get very familiar with the company. Important areas to learn about are; the business operations, culture, financial performance, public announcements, etc. You can review the website, social media pages of the company and consult your professional network for all these details. The company's Annual Report is a great source to get a deeper understanding of functions and financial stability.

REVIEW THE ROLE

Research the role you are interviewing for by thoroughly reviewing the job description. Get a complete overview of what duties, responsibilities and skills are required for the job. Write down your specific experiences which correlate with the requirements of the job. This will allow you to present yourself as the candidate with the most relevant experience that coincides with the role.

PRACTICE WITH A MOCK INTERVIEW

Conduct a practice interview with a friend in order to verbalize your answers, work on body language and gain comfortability with your cadence and flow. This will also help put you at ease and better prepare for potential challenges that you may encounter on the day of the interview. Ask them for critical feedback, incorporate it and practice again.

When you're practicing your interview, it's important to practice in the format that you know the interview will be given. For example, if it's going to be a video call, practice your interview with a friend in the same format. If there's going to be a panel that you're interviewing with, ask a few friends to come over and practice as a group. It can be especially nerve-racking to interview in front of multiple people, so the more comfortable you are with it, the better.

PREPARE QUESTIONS FOR THE INTERVIEWER

Asking pertinent and relevant questions to the interviewer when given a chance is highly important and should be prepared in advance. Do not ask more than 2-3 questions. The goal is not to stomp or outsmart the interviewer. Remember, you are still being assessed during this time. Here are a few examples of possible questions:

- What are successful characteristics of someone in this position?
- What are current challenges for the company/team/position?
- What do you enjoy most about working for this organization?

LOOK THE PART

Plan out your attire for the interview in advance. Attire should be professional (business formal is standard) in most cases however, you can ask the recruiter during the scheduling of the interview.

The night before your interview, iron and lay out your outfit. You should have a back up outfit just in case the one you go for has a stain or tear.

PLAN THE COMMUTE/VIDEO CALL

It is important to arrive at your interview location at least 15 minutes before the interview so plan out your commute and account for potential delays.

If the interview is being conducted virtually then arrange the requirements for video call and check for proper background, lighting, mic and internet connection. Test your technology prior to the interview and log on to the interview platform 5 minutes ahead of schedule.

EXHIBIT POSITIVE BODY LANGUAGE

Your body language can have a significant impact on how you're perceived. During the interview avoid lazy posture or slouching, crossing arms and becoming restless. Try to maintain eye contact and smile and nod where appropriate.

RESPOND TRUTHFULLY AND CONFIDENTLY

Answer the questions asked by the interviewer in a positive tone exhibiting confidence and truthfulness. If you do not know an answer to a question, tell the interviewer that you are unsure, but you will find out and follow up.

Keep answers short, crisp and focused. Back them with your accomplishments and remember your STAR Interview responses!

THANK YOU EMAIL

Send a 'thank you' email either on the same day or within 3 days of the interview thanking the interviewer(s) for the opportunity.

COMMON INTERVIEW MISTAKES

One of the most important parts of interview preparation is also knowing what not to do. People who are conducting interviews are going to notice everything about you from head to toe.

Part of being a professional in any aspect of life is understanding what not to do and what mistakes to avoid. Most people (hopefully) learn from their own mistakes. I have curated this list of common interview mistakes through personal experiences, the experiences of my colleagues, and the things I have seen while conducting interviews myself. Those who have come before all of these mistakes (and more) for you to learn from so that you can deliver a perfect interview and get the job.

1. Being late (virtual or in-person)
2. Poor or weak introduction
3. Failure to research the company
4. Talking too much
5. Badmouthing your past employer
6. Not engaging

BEING LATE

There aren't excuses for showing up to a job interview late, and certainly not for virtual job interviews.

When you head to an in-person interview, you should always plan on arriving to the interview location 10 to 15-minutes early. Depending on the parking situation, you might want to plan on arriving up to 30-minutes early. If you luck out and find a close parking spot with plenty of time to spare, practice your elevator pitch and your STAR Interview Response

Methods. Set a timer for 15 minutes before your interview time, so you have plenty of time to walk to the location.

POOR INTRODUCTION

This is exactly why cultivating your elevator pitch is so important to the success of your interview. Once you've got your 90-second introduction down pat, it will keep working for you every time you use it – in other interviews, networking and social events, when you start a new position and introduce yourself to colleagues, and more.

FAILURE TO RESEARCH THE COMPANY

You've already learned how to properly research a company so this should come easily to you. Pour over their website and social media accounts and commit the job description to memory. If the company is publicly traded, check out their most recent earnings call, too. This will help you craft thoughtful questions and is sure to impress the interviewer.

Interviewers want to know that you're applying for that specific position because you truly have a vested interest in the company. All too often applicants walk in the door because they think they've got the skills and they need a job. However, those kinds of applicants don't usually have longevity within a company because they've applied for the wrong reasons. Your genuine interest in a company will grab the interviewer's attention right off the bat.

TALKING TOO MUCH

You're probably very anxious for the interviewer to get to know you and all of your qualifications, but you should remember to take it slow. Talking too much and oversharing could overwhelm the interviewer or not give them a chance to ask everything they need to. You might think that you've shared all of the most pertinent information about yourself but that's really up to the interviewer. If you don't allow them to get a word in, you'll never be able to know what they're looking for.

Your initial introduction should be 90-seconds or less, and each power story should be 3-minutes or less.

BADMOUTHING YOUR PAST EMPLOYER

If you left a company on bad terms (or are planning to because you just can't stand it anymore), and someone asks you why you parted ways, your first response might be to say something bad about them. However, that is what your friends are for and not your prospective employer.

Instead of focusing on what the company did wrong, focus on your goals and desires. Explain to the interviewer that you are looking for XYZ out of a position and that is what led you on this job search. Always frame the job hunt around yourself rather than past employers.

NOT ENGAGING

Interviews can certainly be anxiety-inducing but that is why there must be plenty of preparation on your part before the big day. Clamming up will not leave a good impression on the interviewer or make them excited to work with you. They are looking for a team member that they can get to know, learn to like, and grow to trust. It's important to showcase that you can rise to the occasion by being engaging and personable.

FOLLOW-UP QUESTIONS

More than likely, your interview is going to end with the question, "what questions do you have for me?" with the expectation that the candidate will come prepared with 2-3 questions for the interviewer.

One of the biggest mistakes that you can make in an interview is leaving without asking them any questions in return. An interview is meant to be a two-way street! You're there to get to know the company and the way it functions just as much as they are there to learn about how you would function within the company.

If you're stumped on where to start when thinking about what questions you would ask someone that is interviewing you, begin by looking at your current or past position. Point out to yourself the things that you like and dislike and ask your interviewer how their company goes about those topics.

For example, perhaps your current boss hosts Monday morning meetings to discuss the week's tasks and Friday afternoon meetings to wrap everything up. If this is something you really like, you could say, "I really liked having two opportunities a week to make sure all of the members in my team are on the same page. What is the communication strategy here?"

Here are a few other sample follow-up questions to ask an interviewer:

- What are the characteristics of an ideal member of your team?
- What do the career paths look like for someone in this position?
- In your opinion, what are the most critical skills for thriving at this company?
- What is your favorite part about working for this company?
- What does a typical day in this position look like?

These questions should give you a real taste of what it's like to be a member of this company's team. They'll also give you a chance to get to know your leader better and see if they are someone that you want to follow. If they answer the last questions by saying that they'll likely be doing the same thing that they're doing today, that might be a red flag that there's stagnation in the company and not a ton of growth opportunities.

The littlest things can make or break an interview. You might leave feeling like you've absolutely crushed it only to never hear from the hiring manager again. Let me walk you through the interview scoring process so that you can really know what's going on in their heads while they interview you and after you leave.

Chapter 6:

SCORING DEMYSTIFIED

"Limitations live only in our minds. But if we use our imaginations, our possibilities become limitless."

—JAMIE PAOLINETTI

These days, it's common practice for interviews to be structured and scored. It sounds a little scary to think that you're sitting there and being scored as you speak but knowing the process will help to ease some of the anxiety that you might feel going into a structured interview.

On the opposite page, you will find an example scoring sheet that includes the following:

- A rating system that is consistent throughout the process
- Specific ways of measuring one's skills, traits, qualifications, and experience
- A section for comments
- A total score

Structuring interviews this way helps to make sure that each and every candidate is evaluated in a similar manner that is fair and consistent across the board. The scoring sheet was created to be completely objective and help decision-makers to compare qualified candidates efficiently.

As you go through the process and give the interviewer your best power stories by using the STAR method format, they will mark the card as they see fit based on your answers. As you can see with this sample scoring sheet, certain answers will be weighed more heavily than others – your interviewer will likely have core competencies that they value more than others. As a candidate you may not know which those are, that's why it's important to come well prepared and avoid making up answers in the moment.

SAMPLE SCORING SHEET

INTERVIEW ASSESSMENT

Candidate:		Date:	
Position:		Interviewer:	

Scoring Key	
Rating	Description
5	Demonstrates **exceptional** understanding of competency
4	Demonstrates **above average** understanding of competency
3	Demonstrates **acceptable** understanding competency
2	Demonstrates **minimal** understanding competency
1	Demonstrates **poor** understanding of competency

Question	Competencies	Score	Weight	Weighted Score
1	Subject Matter Expertise "A"		1	
2	Subject Matter Expertise "B"		1	
3	Subject Matter Expertise "C"		1	
4	Subject Matter Expertise "D"		2	
5	Behavioral Skill #1		1	
6	Behavioral Skill #2		1	
7	Leadership Essentials		2	
8	Leadership Essentials		1	
	Total Score			

Points Earned	What This Means
40 - 50	Congrats! You are a total badass and have positioned yourself as a top contender for the position.
30 - 39	You did a good job in the interview and showcased some potential to perform the essential functions of the job.
0 - 29	I'm afraid you provided little or no evidence of your transferrable skills and are not deemed suitable for this particular role.
Overall Comments (If any)	

POST-INTERVIEW SELF-ASSESSMENT

Some companies aren't as diligent with following up to provide feedback to candidates not selected for the role. This often leaves candidates unsure of their shortcomings and what they could have done differently. With insight into the scoring process and a sample scorecard to go off of, you now have the ability to conduct your own self-assessment following your interview.

It's best practice to write down as many things as you can remember about your interview and conduct the self-assessment right away. This will ensure that your answers – and the experience as a whole – are fresh in your mind.

In addition to the scorecard, consider these factors:

- The experiences and skills that you wanted to highlight vs. what you were able to discuss – did you communicate your talents to the best of your ability? If your intentions and actions don't line up, you know what to focus on when you practice for the next interview.
- Your follow up questions for the interviewer. Did they demonstrate a knowledge of the company as well as a genuine interest?
- Your appearance and attitude vs. that of the interviewer and other employees that you met (if any). It's important to present yourself as exactly what they're looking for.
- The overall tone of the interview and how the interviewer responded when you gave your answers. Their body language can be great insight into their thoughts.

Answer honestly and you will be able to gauge how effective you were in matching your answers with the competencies the interviewer was assessing. If not selected or provided feedback, this will help you determine the precise areas that you need to work on before you search for a different position or have another opportunity to interview.

Don't get discouraged if you've passed your self-assessment with flying colors and didn't get the role. Sometimes, other candidates may have provided slightly better examples or connected differently. The above tools and practices will only help you get better at the interviewing practice so that next time, YOU are the winning candidate. Keep learning, keep trying, and keep moving forward.

Alright, we've come to the final phase of the interviewing process: negotiating your salary offer.

Chapter 7:

NEGOTIATING SALARY

"Whether you think you can or think you can't, you are right."

—HENRY FORD

You did it! You've effectively interviewed like a badass and now you're presented with an offer. Before you accept (no matter how excited you are) it's important to validate that you're being compensated appropriately. No matter what the offer on the table looks like, thank them for it and tell them you will review in detail and get back to them within the next 24 business hours.

The truth is, more than half of employers expect you to make a counteroffer and negotiate your salary. Too many people don't realize that employers are going to offer you the amount they think you'll accept. You do not, by any means, have to accept it!

Read through the negotiation process to decide if the offer that you've been presented with is right for you. If not, it's time to make a counteroffer.

THE NEGOTIATION PROCESS

1. CALCULATE YOUR VALUE

Although I know for a fact that you're absolutely priceless, there is a way to calculate your value in the professional world. You might have to do a little bit of research to gather all the information you'll need to determine what is a fair price for what you're offering

- Market average
- Geographic location
- Years of experience
- Education level and achievements
- Career level and achievements
- Skillset
- Certifications

If you find that your value is higher than the one that you've been presented with, review the details of your offer and align them with the research you've completed into your own value.

2. BACK UP YOUR VALUE WITH TALKING POINTS

Coming up with a salary value that is higher than what you're being offered isn't enough to put on the table. You have to be able to explain to your prospective employer why you feel like you deserve it. You don't need to go into too many details but provide them with enough information to help them understand why you value yourself at that salary.

3.   SPEAK CONFIDENTLY

In any type of negotiation, it's important to deliver your points with confidence. When you are confident in your delivery, your prospective employer will be more apt to take what you have to say into consideration. Weak deliveries lose steam and might not be given a second thought. Employers don't want to coax negotiations out of their employees, either. The process would be much easier for them if they don't have to spend time discussing values. If they feel like you aren't even taking yourself seriously when you're negotiating your salary, they most certainly won't.

4.   ALWAYS SHOOT FOR A HIGHER VALUE

Once you've determined the salary you think you deserve, tell the employer you want five percent more than that. After they've tried to negotiate you down, you're more likely to end up with a number you're quite comfortable with. It might even be the ideal salary you had in mind all along.

5.   CONSIDER JOB-RELATED EXPENSES

It's not completely unheard of for candidates to ask potential employers to consider their expenses when determining salary. If you're taking a position that's farther away from home, or one that you have to move for, they might very well take that into consideration and jack up their offer a little bit to meet you in the middle.

6.   BE FLEXIBLE

In many corporate companies, they offer compensation packages that include much more than a base salary. Your total compensation package will be your paycheck plus all of the benefits that come along with being an employee of that specific company. When negotiating your salary, it's important to ask about the total compensation package because you might find the monetary amount acceptable after you factor in all of the other benefits.

There are many areas of compensation that might be in your prospective company's package:

- **Employee profit sharing** – In addition to the offered salary, some companies will offer their employees the opportunity to purchase stock and share in the profits. If the company is successful, you can earn an additional salary

- **Bonuses** – According to Indeed, there are five types of bonuses:
    - Performance-related: when goals are met or exceeded
    - Commissioned: a bonus that is tied to the number of sales you make or the dollar amount of those sales
    - Contracted: when you are in an executive-level position, you are expected to perform at a higher level. Your exact bonus will rely on a determined set of factors and is not always guaranteed. These may include bonuses for loyalty to the company (retention), growth goals, sales, etc. Typically, contracted bonuses are set to be a certain percentage of your total salary and distributed once a year.
    - Non-exempt: overtime pay
    - Situational: holidays and events

- **401k match** – On average, companies that match their employees' 401k will put in 50 percent of every dollar up to 6 percent of the employee's salary. That means a yearly raise of up to 6 percent.

- **Lifestyle benefits** – these include discounts on things like hotels and flights, phone plans, gym memberships, car payments, tolls, parking fees, and more. If your company covers lifestyle costs, consider how that affects your monthly/yearly budget.

- **Professional development** – this includes education, certifications, conferences, etc.
- **Health insurance** – Consider the type of health insurance that's offered and the amount of your premium your company is willing to cover.

7. DON'T BE AFRAID TO SAY NO

You've come too far in life to accept anything less than what you're worth. Denying a job offer might prolong your job search, but you will be in a much better situation than you would be if you accepted the offer and couldn't make ends meet because of it.

Still, there are situations where a job will be worth it even though your paychecks aren't what you want them to be – maybe your new job is less stressful, closer to home, or allows you to work remotely when you can't make it to the office. If you accept based on the non-monetary perks, make sure that it's a decision that you can live with for at least a year or two. "Job hopping" looks poor on a resume – companies look for stability in their candidates and will avoid hiring talent that appears to have short-term intentions for their organization.

Final Thoughts

"Go confidently in the direction of your dreams! Live the life you've imagined."

—HENRY DAVID THOREAU

The interview process is no doubt anxiety-inducing but educating yourself about the things that make you fearful is the first step to overcoming the feeling. I believe that we tend to overcomplicate the interview process because of the importance that the outcome holds. We tend to psych ourselves out, thinking that interviews are meant to test us when, in reality, they are simply a method for you and a company to get to know each other better.

You already have all the magic that you need inside of you; it's time to articulate your talents and show the world that YOU are a badass!

When you find a position and company that aligns with what you want and what you have to offer, you will see that the life of your dreams is just around the corner.

You were born to live a life of abundance. Everything that you could ever want is available to you. You simply need to know where to look and have the determination to acquire it. If you apply for the right positions and leverage the strategies for interviewing like a badass, you're going to be successful. You might even have job offers filling your inbox!

When you recognize your potential, the world will follow suit.

Bonus

7 DONE-FOR-YOU EMAIL SCRIPTS

EMAIL 1 – INTRODUCTION TO RECRUITER BEFORE APPLYING

Subject line: How Can I Make A Difference at [COMPANY NAME]

Dear [RECRUITER NAME]

I have noticed the level of excellence and growth that [COMPANY NAME] has displayed for the past several years. I find this consistency and work culture highly attractive and I'm interested in finding out more about [SPECIFIC DEPARTMENT OR POSITION].

I currently work as a [POSITION] for [TEAM OR COMPANY NAME] and have [NUMBER] years of experience as a [SKILL OR PROFESSION]. I believe our goals and interests are aligned, and with my skills, resources and work ethic we can both accomplish more.

I would love to schedule a time to discuss how we may work together.

Here is my LinkedIn profile [LINK TO PROFILE].

I have also attached my resume for your consideration.

Please let me know what day and time are most convenient for you for this discussion.

Thanks in advance,

[YOUR NAME]

PRO TIP:

Keep your first email short and to the point.

Ensure the deliverables are intact: links should route to the correct profile, your most current resume is attached. You should not follow up to this email to resend documents or correct errors. Leave the scheduling date/time for the recruiter to determine so you do not come off too aggressive.

EMAIL 2 – CONTACTING A RECRUITER AFTER APPLYING TO A POSITION

Subject line: [YOUR NAME] – The Best New Addition to your Team!

Dear [RECRUITER NAME],

While searching for new opportunities within my professional field, I came across a job opening at [COMPANY NAME] for the position of [SPECIFIC ROLE] posted online at, [NAME OF CAREER SITE].

I promptly submitted my application and I'm excited about this role. The position aligns perfectly with my experience and skills in [LIST 1-2 SKILLS RELATED TO THIS POSITION].

I recently followed you on [PLATFORM] and I admire how you interact with candidates and provide valuable resources to job seekers.

I would love to schedule a time to discuss my experience and the value I can bring to this role if given the opportunity. For your convenience, I have re-attached my resume, and here is my LinkedIn profile [LINK PROFILE].

I am available on [WEEKDAYS] any time between [TIME & TIME ZONE] if these times are convenient for you.

I look forward to setting up a preferable meeting time and discussing with you. Thank you!

Sincerely,
[YOUR NAME]

PRO TIP:

Use the job description to make sure the 1-2 skills you list directly align with the position you applied to. Ensure that your most current resume is attached. Test the link to make sure it routes to the correct LinkedIn profile. List a few weekdays for availability. Only include working hours between 9-5 pm local time for your discussion.

EMAIL 3 – FOLLOW UP WITH A RECRUITER TO CHECK THE STATUS OF APPLICATION

Subject line: I'm Checking In!

Hello [RECRUITER NAME]

I hope you are doing well. I can understand how busy you must be during this time and will keep my message brief.

I am a [SKILL OR PROFESSION] at [TEAM OR CURRENT COMPANY] and I recently applied for the position of [SPECIFIC ROLE] at your company, [COMPANY NAME].

I am writing to follow-up on the application and kindly ask if you can provide your decision timeline.

The role of [SPECIFIC POSITION] is one that combines my experience in [RELATED SKILL OR PROFESSION] and I'm truly enthusiastic at the prospect of joining your company for this role. I am ready to help bring my [HOW YOU CAN BENEFIT THE COMPANY] to deliver results and facilitate even more growth in the company.

Please let me know if you require additional information for any stages in the hiring process.

Thank you again for considering my application.

Warm regards,

[YOUR NAME]

PRO TIP:

Recruiters are busy juggling multiple candidates at various stages in many different interview processes. It is ok to check in. Most often this could serve as a prompt for the recruiter to follow up with the hiring manager. If you do not receive a response, consider this lead a dead end and do not continue to reach out.

EMAIL 4 – REACHING OUT TO YOUR PROFESSIONAL NETWORK ON LINKEDIN

Subject line: I Need Your Help!

Hello [NAME],

I hope you are doing well! I recently began my search for a new career opportunity within the [PROFESSION] field. It has been both inspiring and beneficial working at [CURRENT EMPLOYER] as their [CURRENT ROLE] for the last [LENGTH OF TIME]. But at the moment, I'm looking for a new role to challenge me, engage my experience and resources, and help me grow.

Thankfully, I came across an open position for [SPECIFIC JOB TITLE] at [COMPANY NAME]. I wanted to reach out to see if you can connect to someone in the hiring department for this role.

Your assistance is greatly appreciated, and I will be glad to provide any details that can help. Thank you!

Warm regards,

[YOUR NAME]

PRO TIP:

This is someone you know, but do not add additional topics in this email. Keep it solely focused on the referral and you can engage in more personal dialog in subsequent correspondence.

EMAIL 5 – THANK YOU EMAIL TO PROFESSIONAL NETWORK

Subject line: You Deserve a Medal.

Hello [NAME],

I hope you are having a great week. I wanted to extend my appreciation for your assistance recently. Thank you for helping me connect with the hiring team and passing on my resume for consideration.

I am excited about this potential opportunity and I'm waiting patiently to hear back from the hiring team. Hopefully, its good news!

Whichever way, thank you again for your help and I hope to talk again soon.

Best wishes,

[YOUR NAME]

PRO TIP:

Always circle back and thank your referral. This is not a personal email so make sure you keep the focus on your job search and reserve more personal notes for emails to follow.

Only provide one follow up to your referral unless they reach out for more updates. You do not want to place any burden or undue hardship on your network. Their role is strictly to pass along your resume or hand you off to the hiring manager. Do not damage your connection by continuing to solicit insight that they might not have.

EMAIL 6 – THANK YOU EMAIL TO INTERVIEWERS

Subject line: Thank You, [INTERVIEWER'S NAME]

Hello [INTERVIEWER'S NAME],

Thank you so much for taking the time to connect with me yesterday and share your valuable time and insights. It was great to hear about the company's goals, culture, the role, and expectations. [COMPANY NAME] does seem like a wonderful place to work and not just because of the [PERK MENTIONED DURING THE INTERVIEW].

Our conversation about [1 SPECIFIC TOPIC] has made me even more excited about this role and given me a better insight into what it would be like to join the company.

From our conversation, I picked out [1 PARTICULAR INSIGHT SHARED] and have begun working on something similar. Thank you for that!

Please let me know if you need anything else for the remaining stages of the hiring process.

I hope to hear back from you soon.

Thanks again for your time.

Regards,
[YOUR NAME]

This is the most critical email you will send through the job search process. Take good notes during your interview as it will come in handy here. You want to pack in 2 to 3 key discussion points from your conversation to show your level of engagement.

EMAIL 7 – NO OFFER EXTENDED RESPONSE

Subject line: Rare Talent Signing Off...

Dear [RECRUITER'S NAME],

I hope this message finds you well. I wanted to say thank you for considering my application and it was indeed wonderful to have gained further insight into the company's goals and expectations.

While I'm disappointed to discover I was not selected for the position of [JOB TITLE], I did enjoy the opportunity to be interviewed for the role.

I would love to hear your feedback concerning my interview and application. Any details you can provide might prove helpful for my future endeavors and ongoing job search.

I do hope to connect again soon and would greatly appreciate being considered for any future job openings at your company.

Thank you again for your time. My best wishes to you and the rest of the team.

Warmest regards,

[YOUR NAME]

PRO TIP:

Always follow up when you do not get the position. Any feedback you can gain from this experience will only help you better prepare for your next one.

Also, you never know; the top candidate could fall through or additional positions may become available. Do not let your ego get the best of you here. Your final email could be a game-changer and help keep you top of mind in the future.

*How to
Interview Like a
Badass*

WORKBOOK

01

Worksheet One

Doing your research and knowing a bit about the company is a basic expectation of recruiters and hiring managers. The goal of this worksheet is to help you capture information on a company during the job search process.

Do Your Research

What is the company's mission, vision, values and current performance? Find all current information on the company and the position you applied to.

- Class of 2024 med school demo 25.7% underrepresented minority
- Student Org: Pride, Latino Medical Student Association, Student National Medical Assoc
Future doctors Pipel

Goal timeline:

Due date:

02

COMPENTENCY ALIGNMENT

Grab a copy of the job description for the position your are interested in. Use this worksheet to identify the key competencies required for this position and align with times when you have demonstrated these in your current or previous role. This will help you assess compatibility for the role and lay the foundation for your Power Stories.

Key Competencies: List key skills the company has outlined on the job description. e.g. "manage execution"

Experiences: Identify examples where you have demonstrated this competency successfully. e.g. "holiday reset at Walmart"

KEY COMPETENCIES	EXPERIENCES
Scheding of events Day to Day Ops implementation	
Disseminates info to medical students regarding scholarships, internships, summer programs,	
Develop surveys to excess experience of student & mentor	
Supervise oversee admin staff	
Maintain & monitor monthly budget - Develop new programing to address needs - web page oversee	
Recruitment Medical School fairs at high school & colleges	

Worksheet Three

03

TELL ME ABOUT YOURSELF? THE KEY TO NAILING YOUR INTRODUCTION

The goal of this worksheet is to help you craft the details to include in your 90 second elevator pitch to introduce yourself and share a brief overview of your experience. Combine your notes from each section to create a script in chapter 3 that flows.

Question one - where did you grow up? Where did you go to school? What did you study? Did you have an extracurricular activities while in school?

Question two - what experience do you have? Provide a high level walk through of your resume. Explain your role(s) in 1-2 sentences. Call out key responsibilities as it relates to the role you are interviewing for.

Question three - what do you do when you are not working? List volunteer work, hobbies, interests, etc. This should be something they will remember about you.

04

CLEARLY ARTICULATE YOUR EXPERIENCE USING THE STAR METHOD

The key to nailing behavioral-based questions is to determine Power Stories that can address the preferred skills listed in the job positing. Use your experiences identified in worksheet 2 and follow steps 1-4 for each.

Step one - State the situation in 1-2 sentences. Set up the story as an overview of the problem.

Step two - Describe the specific challenge or task that relates to the question and your responsibility in the situation.

Step three - What did you do the resolve the issue? Share your actions and behaviors, who you partnered with and what resources were leveraged.

Step four - End with the results of the situation. The more measurable the result the better. If the result was not favorable or too recent to measure - do not use this power story.

SITUATION	TASK	ACTIONS	RESULTS

05

Worksheet Five

INTERVIEW PREP CHECKLIST

Dedicate at least one hour a day studying the information you have entered in this workbook. Use this checklist to stay organized.

ITEMS TO REVIEW

About the Author

Latoya Baldwin is a passionate career woman, devoted mother, and total badass.

Latoya earned her B.S. in Finance from the University of Tennessee at Chattanooga and pivoted from the banking industry to retail management. Early in her career, she realized that her magic was in aligning people strategies to business objectives, and she dove right into human resources.

Through the years, she has served as a business partner supporting global initiatives for several Fortune 40 companies, been a trusted advisor to senior leaders with tens of thousands of employees and assisted with a $60M HR transformation that deployed talent recruitment strategies for over 3 million annual applicants.

Her success and insight into corporate America coupled with the devastating impact that COVID-19 had on the job market spurred Latoya into action. Realizing that she had the opportunity and ability to help others energize their careers, she created her self-empowerment brand, Latoya Baldwin.

To find additional resources and actionable career advice please visit www.latoyabaldwin.com.